20 ways to increase Sperm Count naturally

DR.M.HAINDAVI

20 Ways to increase SPERM COUNT Naturally
(Say Good Bye to Male Infertility)

Author:
DR. HAINDAVI MANTHANI
MD Ayurveda

First edition
2020

About the author

The author Dr.M.Haindavi MD Ayurveda has done her post-graduation in Prasuthi Tantra & Stree Roga and her research specialisation was regarding Infertility. She is a recipient of Pratibha Awardee, Ayurvisharadha awardee and has secured a position in Indian book of records in 2019.

First edition: **2020**
Copyrights reserved:
© **Dr.Haindavi Manthani**

Write to us:
drchittymanthena@gmail.com

PREFACE

I am glad to bring forward the book that is entitled '20 ways to Increase the Sperm Count Naturally'. This book is a sum up of all the essential lifestyle modifications that a person should implement in his daily routine in order to be fertile and thus he will be very capable to impregnate his partner. My idea to combine the Ayurveda remedies that were described in this book will surely help the needy. Many people are in search of the helping guidelines to be followed naturally rather than going to the hospitals and the medications. So I thought this book of tips and tricks will surely help those people.

DR.M.HAINDAVI
MD Ayurveda

Contents

INTRODUCTION

Welcome to the book of reality and the extremely useful content of the Male Community. Here we have tried to elaborate the essential useful tips and information that really helps you to Increase your Sperm Count Naturally without any interference with Medications or the Injections.

You have ended up into the Book of Lifestyle Management in order to Generate New Healthy Sperms by yourself and to eliminate all the dead and crooked sperms outside. Don't miss any part of the book dear. You can also have the Ayurveda way of managing your sexual life to produce a very healthy baby of yours by knowing every part of the book.

Let's go into the detail of the book.........

1. FREQUENT EJACULATION

Many people consider it as a myth and don't follow it properly. The thing is that some people, who are trying to impregnate their wife, think that the Frequent Ejaculation will result in the substantial increase of the Sperm Count Naturally and they do follow it but fail at the successful rates of the Pregnancy.

We are not here to talk about the general population of Male who are not concerned with or who are not in the line of fertility way. They are free of the rules of their frequency of their Ejaculation. But the people who are already Sub-Fertile and fail repeatedly in the conception must follow the guidelines of their frequency.

People who have a very good Sperm Count are free to take their ejaculation very number of times but to make a quality point they need to wait for some days before they go to their partner.

If you think about the case of testing your semen analysis when suggested by the Andrologist or the doctor you concerned to deal your infertility, you are suggested to wait for at least 2-3 days and ask to maintain abstinence for the appropriate period and then go for the test so that the test results will be very accurate.

Then when you are going to give life to a new one then what's wrong to wait for certain period to maintain the quality of the Semen *'The life content of your body'*.

We generally recommend you to wait and take at least a gap of 3 days every time you make with your wife.

Because a time period of 3 days will sum up your semen volume to bring you an increased content of the semen along with the increased count of your sperms.

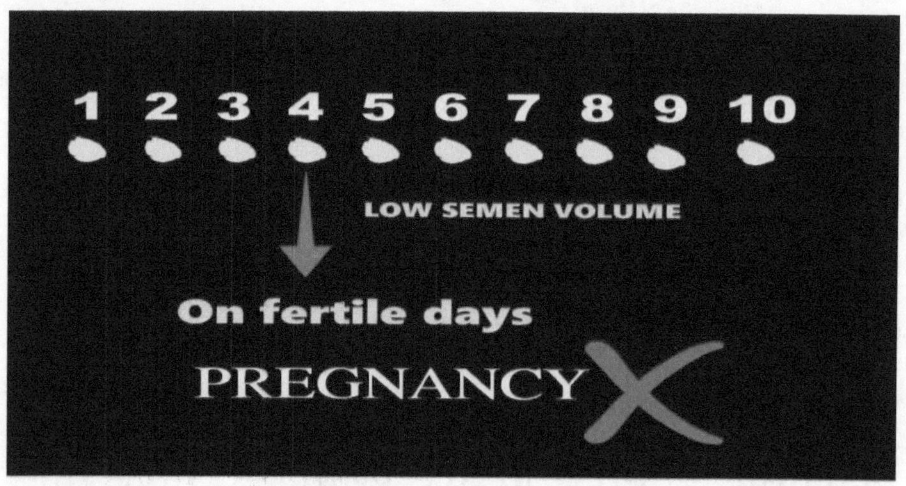

If we consider a person who is habituated to ejaculate his semen on a regular daily basis or more even often in a single day, then on the fertile days of his wife, he is able to produce only a very low volume of semen which will not be sufficient to impregnate her, hence he fails often.

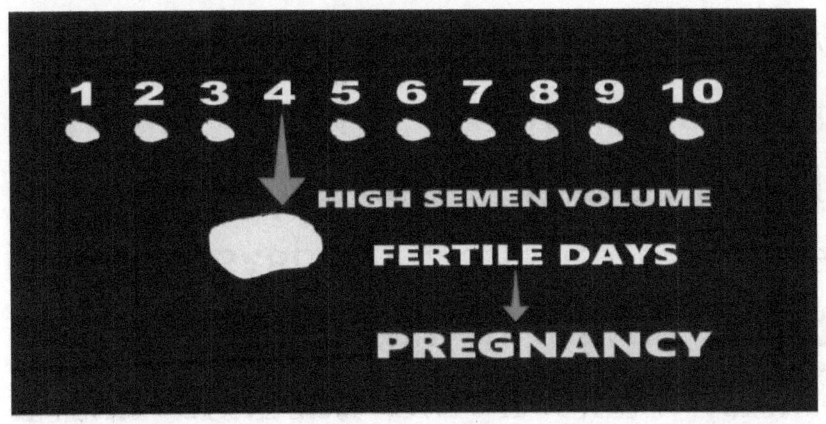

On contrary, if a person waits for 3 days and then tries on her fertile days then, he will have a more accumulated content of the semen with an increased count of his sperms which is more than normal and sufficient to impregnate his wife and then he succeeds to be fertile.

Also if a couple is seriously trying for baby, then they have to check the fertile days of the woman and if they could anticipate the fertile days, then it is better to stay abstinence for 4 days before the fertile period and then it is advised to have intercourse for higher chances of fertility.

The couple is suggested to have an intercourse on alternate days in times of fertile days if he has a low count or on daily basis if the husband has a sufficient amount of sperm count.

If the wife is monitored on USG, ultrasound for the ovulation day and is promptly known of that day, they can have their intercourse by the guidance of the radiologist and the gynaecologist accordingly.

Also according to Ayurveda, the husband should not indulge in any kind of masturbation or the ejaculation by other means and should be in *Brahmacharya*' absolutely when not being with his wife. Hope you understand what the actual meaning it has in depth.

It's better to avoid indulging with other woman by all means. It is an unhealthy habit which results in many kinds of Genital Diseases which can then may lead to Male Infertility. Non-natural methods for Ejaculation are not considered safe and not recommended anytime. If you follow these advices like avoiding frequent ejaculation and also avoiding masturbation, then you can have an increase in your sperm count naturally.

2. TOO LONG GAP

Many people also think that if they will not meet for many days then they could easily make up with the high amount of the semen volume which then can be used during the fertile days of the wife for impregnation.

Also in many couple situations, the wife will be in one place for the sake of taking fertility treatment and the husband will be in other place for the job sake or other reason. The husband comes to his wife when the doctor suggests to have an intercourse according by the sonography suggested ovulation days of the women.

But the thing is that the husband is not indulged in any kind of ejaculatory process throughout the 20 days or a little less since the previous month. Here in this case as the semen was stored in the genitals for such a long time, then there are chances for the sperms to undergo the oxidative stress and thereby the sperms get damaged and die in the organs.

So a sperm content that is rich in dead sperms will be used during the ovulatory period of the wife and then the entire effort made for the fertility treatment get ruined.

A fresh content with good semen quality is not being used in this case. Hence a person should remember to get eliminate his stored semen once every 7 days in order to get a fresh and quality semen to impregnate his wife. At least this should be done 1 week before the fertile days of the wife. It's just like an example that the running car will be in condition than the car that is just kept for show purpose.

The more time the sperm stay in the testes, the more chances to undergo for the oxidative stress. This kind of sexual behaviour may help you in preventing the prostate cancer in future.

This on and off methods along with ovulation predictor kits will help you to get a baby soon. More than a count matter, you need to have a very healthy sperms for a healthy baby. This is possible by following these methods.

The older sperms begin to die within the body if not ejaculated and could sum up with the freshly formed sperms.

That unhealthy composition of semen is not that efficient to get a healthy baby. The immotile sperms percentage will be high in the ejaculations that are very infrequent.

Even if you want to test your semen for analysis, the doctor advices you to get a sample that is not older than 7 days. An important point to be remembered to have an increased sperm count naturally.

3. OVER THE COUNTER

There are many available Testosterone supplements in the market and can be available over the counter. Because of the high marketing of these products which are available in the injection form or gel, people have become most aware of these products.

Many people are habituated to get them by the counter and use them to boost the Testosterone levels in their body. In order to make up the Drive, Mood, Musculature, Energy and Vitality, these are used in a variety of forms. When it comes to the people with infertility, its use should be limited and especially a big NO'.

Some people may think that the immediate increase of the hormone levels in their body could resolve all their infertility problems and could also flare up their sperm count by no time. But that's not the Truth.

These habits and practices can cause more harm than doing good to your body. So, one should remember that the medications & the supplements of the Testosterone should always be prescribed by the Registered Medical Practitioner like the concerned Gynaecologist or the Andrologist.

The habit of taking over the counter Testosterone hormone will hamper the production of the Natural Hormone that is produced in your body.

Hence there should not be any artificial thing that can ruin your natural one. Doctor generally advice you to take this supplement when your body fails to produce the hormone in sufficient.

In cases of hypo-gonadism, it is used in order to make the hormone replacement. But these when taken in excess amounts have higher risk for the health of the person. The man is at greater risk of heart problems and prostate issues.

Most important thing to remember is that if your body is habituated to the external source of the testosterone, then your body stops producing of its own in a period later.

People should not be treated on their own but instead always follow the instructions of the doctor. Not only the testosterone, should you not take any kind of medications for any kind of illness.

Many medications have their effect on your reproductive system and some are even capable to kill your sperms.

So hence it's better not to take medication by your own but instead follow the diet and other habits to increase the sperm count and motility.

4. TIGHT DRESS

Even a dress that you wear decides your fertility levels that you internally possess especially in cases of men. It starts early in your teens. Hence be careful if you have a habit of wearing a Tight Outfit in and out such as a tight innerwear or any kind of tight skinny jeans.

The male reproductive system is hence designed in such a way that the external Genital Organs should hang outside a little away from the body so that to maintain the appropriate lower temperature that is required for the spermatogenesis and for the healthy sperm production.

But if your lifestyle and your dressing will keep your external genitals too close to your body, that too for a very longer time periods in duration of the day, then it surely adversely effects the production of sperms as the temperature of scrotal sac increases.

Generally the internal body temperature is higher than the external Genitals of Male but by being closer to the body parts, the Genitals may heat up & thus the sperms may get damaged and their motility may also be affected.

As per the South Indian tradition the males when have a habit of wearing a loose lower wear like Dhothi' or Lungi' or Pancha' then it will be apt to maintain the health status of the genitals. This kind of dressing style or habit along with a loose inner garment provides you proper air circulation to your genitals and helps to maintain lower temperature.

Also people who wear the tight outfit have their obstruction to the blood flow and thus adversely affect the health of the external parts.

Also the tight garments can cause pressure over the body and may encourage breeding of the bacteria & fungi thus causing the fungal infections in the Genital Parts. It then causes further infections.

If the increased temperature has interrupted the sperm production in the testicles, it leads to lower sperm count with low motility. It's very important to reduce the heat stress over Genitals in order to resume the normal sperm production. The men are also advised to wear a loose outfit like trousers while trying to impregnate his wife to boost up the sperm count.

Also the cotton innerwear is advised rather than the synthetic wear as they trap heat inside causing harm to the gametes.

These synthetic materials may also cause heavy sweating leading to much kind of infections thereby. The dress must be cotton and breathable allowing proper air circulation to the external genital parts.

So, you have learned how a simple change in your dress pattern can affect the reproductive health of a person. Many researchers have also found the effect of colour of the dress over the sperm count of a person.

You can't believe the results that the people who have a habit of wearing black jeans have low sperm count rather than the people with a habit of wearing blue jeans. So the colour of your dress also matters.

If you realise the content and want to switch your dressing style then you are in a right path, you can reverse your low count and increase the sperm count naturally by this change.

5. RADIATION

Radiation is hazardous to health anyways but in specific it causes potential harm to the sperms in means of damaging their DNA material and hampering their motility too.

Many men have habit of keeping their mobile phones in the jeans pocket in a regular basis which can cause radiation effect over their genital parts continuously. It also affects the people who are working with computers and laptops and have a habit of keeping their laptop in their laps while working on it.

The phone radiation will adversely affect the volume of the semen content along with the sperm count number, its motility, viability of the sperms and finally it effects the fertility of the male leading to infertility problems.

It entirely comes under the lifestyle concerns because of the raise of mobile phones and laptops in this generation and era. People who are exposed to radiation in means of phone calls either in the talk mode or stand by, Wi-Fi or other ways have higher chances of getting the DNA fragmentation in their sperm cells.

The motility is also adversely effected which in turns fail at the time fertilisation to reach the egg in the female genital tract. Along with the disturbed spermatogenesis the electromagnetic radiation also causes various health issues in a person like genital tumours, prostate cancer etc.

Many researchers have been done with this topic by taking separate groups and have concluded that the people who had more talk over the phone directly are less affected but the people who kept the phones in the pocket closer to their testicles while in the talk mode by using a headset or Bluetooth may have higher chances of damaging their anti-oxidants which are very useful in preventing the oxidative stress damage of the sperms. This leads to the higher chances of damaging the sperms.

In turn, it finally causes Low Sperm Count in that person. Also, using a laptop in the laps created more heat around the Genital parts. It's already known fact that the high temperature is not suitable for the spermatogenesis.

It has been found that the organs cannot resume the production of the sperms until the temperature has been to the normal stage. So, it has been the primary reason for making more males of this generation infertile. A simple change of lifestyle by making simple changes can take back your damage.

Limiting your phone calls and laptop use can bring you the normal production of sperms. A quality of the semen is also maintained thereafter for sure. You must remember not to keep the phone in the lower pocket anytime or at least not more than 4hrs continuously. You should make a habit of carrying it in other bag or pouch kept in the car or bike while travelling and on the table or drawer while working at the office. You should keep your phone at a larger distance while sleeping. Keeping the phone in any other room but not in your bedroom is a good option.

The long hours of night in the resting stage is to repair & relax your body. It's very important to keep your surroundings calm and healthy, free of any kind of radiation all the night. This habit increases your Sperm Count naturally.

6.DRUG ABUSE

A substance abuse or drug abuse can ruin your reproductive health and cause male infertility. If a person is addicted to any kind of drugs such as opiates, tobacco or steroids it can adversely affect his health. The high cravings of the drug and a repeated use of those can damage many organs and systems in the body along with the reproductive organs.

The marijuana, cocaine like substances can damage the organs and affect the size of the Testis. The person who has drug abuse to narcotics has higher chances to develop the hypogonadism which can cause all hormonal disturbances in his body leading to Male Infertility. If the abuse is continued for longer periods the Genitals can also be subjected to cancers leading to Testicular Cancer.

The cells are intensely damaged to perform their normal function i.e. to produce the sperms. This leads to lower your Sperm Count levels and their motility.

The active component of the marijuana can lower the levels of your testosterone and thus weakens your sexual drive too. Whatever the impact, the final result is Impotency or Infertility.

Whether these legal or illegal drugs were used by a person for a short span or longer periods, the results would be damaging only. Hence it's better to control your senses & cravings to stop all these addictions at least when you are serious about becoming a father.

Because you should feel responsibility to give birth to a healthy baby as all these Drug Abuse can lead to DNA damage of your sperms thereby the babies born to you will be unhealthy with many Genetic Disorders.

In order to increase your sperm count you need to stop all these substance abuse. Also, if you are suffering from any kind of illnesses and are under medication for your illness on a daily basis, then you must remember to consult a fertility expert in order to enquire whether you can continue those medications while trying to father a child or not.

The reason behind this is that some kind of medications can really hamper your sperm production in your organs and can cause Low Sperm Count. Hence it is very important to stop all kind of medications, drugs, substances, and any form of things that are taken in a daily basis in order to maintain the quality of the semen and the quantity of the sperms.

Stopping all those addictions will surely increase your sperm count naturally.

7. POLLUTION AND CHEMICALS

In this present situation there has been raise in the pollution levels in the air. The air we breathe decides the health status of an individual. Researchers have found that the air pollution is linked with the DNA changes of the sperm in the males thus leading to Low Sperm Count in a person.

With the increasing industries and urbanization, the air pollution has been substantially increased in all countries. The heavy metals in the air like lead, mercury etc. are potent enough to decrease the Motility of the sperms.

So, the person seeking infertility treatment should be cautious, better not to expose to traffic pollutants while going outside and should wear protective mask to prevent the pollutants to get inhaled.

Also the people who are forced to the Traffic Pollutants by occupation should take required precautions. Also the use of pesticides and the chemicals have its adverse effect on the reproductive organs. All the people who are occupationally concerned with these kind of chemical substances in their work area, pesticides use by the farmers and people who work in the agriculture, people who are exposed to the industrial waste products both solid and gaseous, have higher chances to have fertility problems. As we cannot suggest you to change your occupation as it is your only way to earn your butter and bread but you should be cautious while working and being in those places.

Taking proper care while handling will increase your sperm count. Also the men should be very careful while using their cosmetics and the perfumes.

For the fragrance and beauty means, if a person over uses the cosmetics and certain kind of perfumes, the harmful chemicals that were used in these substances can reach your reproductive organs to damage your cells that are involved in making and producing your gametes, the sperms.

Many research studies have found that the chemicals used in the cosmetics can lower the Sperm Count, can lower the motility of the sperms, and can degrade them in preventing the progressive movement of the sperms too there by affecting the fertile aspect of that person.

So, it's better to stay away from all these chemicals, pesticides, beauty products, perfumes etc. It's the better way to increase your sperm count naturally.

8.HOT BATHS

Some changes in the habits and practices in your daily life will surely give you the better results of your health when seriously implemented. Men should avoid the hot baths especially the hot tub baths exposing the external genitals to high temperature for long times.

As the high temperature gives you the risk of decreasing the Sperm Count and also hampers the production of the sperms, the hot water dribbling over the parts should be avoided.

Also, the excess steam baths repeatedly and frequently exposes the testicles to high temperature which is also not a healthy habit for the people who really want to father a child.

However the condition caused by these hot baths is reversible. But the people who already have a very little count, they should be careful regarding these sauna baths. The time spent in the hot tubs is directly proportional to the lowering of the sperm count.

Already researches have been done to the people who are habituated to take hot tub baths. They have learned that the high temperatures are potent enough to kill the sperms leading to the lower sperm count & defective sperm function. But don't worry, the condition can be reversible when the person shuts off this habit for some days.

So always remember to maintain a normal temperature at your external organs to allow its natural function of spermatogenesis and don't ever interfere its function by your faulty practices.

You may not know what the real cause that made you infertile is. Just leaving away this habit can improve your Sperm Count Naturally.

9.ALCOHOL

Many men have a habit of taking the alcohol as a party basis, some in a regular basis and a few in a daily basis. No matter how frequent you take but the alcohol is well known hazardous to your health.

When you can't maintain a proper health of your internal organs by the habit of taking alcohol how can you think to give birth to a healthy offspring.

The genital organs are also prone to the harmful effects of the alcohol. Also as the liver is damaged by the excess alcoholism, the proteins required to bind the sex hormones is lowered.

Also, research studies show evidences of lowering the testosterone hormone in the body for the people who are addicted to the alcohol.

When your body is not enough to maintain the proper and normal levels of the hormone then how one can produce the required amount of the sperms that are required for the impregnation of your partner?

Alcohol intake is potent enough to alter the shape of the normal structure of the sperms, their motility and their viability. Hence people with alcohol intake have Lower Sperm Count. Heavy alcohol intake can hamper the hormone levels in the Male like it interferes with FSH, LH, and testosterone levels in the body.

The occasional alcohol drink is unlikely to affect the health of an individual but the people who are heavy drinkers, the reproductive health is very deteriorated. A woman cares her baby since she becomes pregnant and even after delivery, she has to eat and lead a life that is compatible to the baby. A long time she is spending in care of your offspring.

Then why can't you manage yourself for some months. It's your responsibility to produce a healthy sperm for the Fertilization in order to have a healthy baby. Just be *satwik*' it means to be a pure soul and discontinue all the faulty habits of your lifestyle and just lead a life of pure and calm which should be healthy.

A few months of stopping all the faulty addictions, your body discards all the unhealthy, dead, immotile and crooked sperms outside of your body by ejaculation and then starts preparing the healthy, potent sperms for the baby you want to create for yourself.

Generally the sperms need 70 days of time to complete their formation. Hence you should plan your baby 2-3 months prior and stop all the addictions and lead a healthy life.

A healthy habit created will not go waste. You will be able to produce healthy, motile sperms with a good genetic material and good morphology and the semen will have a high sperm count with a high motility and viability.

What's wrong in trying this for some months? After all you become healthy individual by repairing all your internal organs along with your reproductive organs.

Then you will surely able to produce the healthy sperms after 2-3 months. A perfect planning will result you a beautiful strong immune baby.

Why the Men community have this alcohol as energy drink?? There are many ways to come out of it right.

A single resolution before your planning surely helps you to increase the Sperm Count Naturally.

10. SMOKING

Smoking is also not a healthy habit as you all know. It damages, not only your respiratory organs, it will affect your reproductive organs too. People with smoking as a habit not only damaging their own health but they are also deteriorating the family member's health by smoking in their own house near them.

But you know you are going to damage the health of your unborn baby too. Because the people whether they are light smokers, moderate smokers or the heavy smokers, their sperms will have the DNA material get damaged.

The smokers will have a very lower sperm count with a low quality semen and sperm. With that damaged part of their sperms if they want to impregnate his partner, the failure rates will be very high to those kinds of people.

Even if unfortunately she gets pregnant by the sperms of that person the chances of miscarriage is very high as the unborn baby may have many kind of genetic problems.

Even if the fetus is not aborted but have sustained the long journey of the total months of pregnancy and born alive, the baby may have many serious illnesses.

What's the mistake of the baby, after all the father is the culprit. He with his addiction of smoking has damaged the health of his baby too in this manner.

Hence a person when seriously trying to father a child, remember one thing that he must quit smoking first and after you be like a good boy, then wait for 3 months to allow your body to discard the unhealthy sperms and your body will get ready to produce the healthy sperms which gives you a healthy child.

You must know that even the IVF success rates are very low for the person who is addicted to smoking.

Research studies show that the smoking adversely effects and lowers the reproductive hormones like FSH and Testosterone in their body which is very essential for the sperm production.

Also the smoking can kill the sperms in the body by increasing the oxidative stress. By the end result the DNA of sperms is damaged resulting in the badly shaped sperms affecting their motility leading to the bad swimmers.

So, make sure to quit this habit before you plan your baby so that to increase the sperm count naturally.

11. MASSAGE

Massage, the ancient method to cure any kind of disease according to Ayurveda. The daily routine must include at least 15-20 minutes of massage with any kind of the herbal oils.

In general we recommend the sesame oil in the absence of herbal oils. The oil must be made lukewarm before the massage. The benefits of the massage are really mind blowing.

In particular if you want to improve your sperm count levels, then it's time to concentrate on your thigh parts.

The massage should be done in upwards direction towards the genitals so as to improve the blood circulation of the genitals which in turn will increase the sperm count for sure. Remember to be very gentle while doing the massage.

Each part of the massage should be 5 minutes each. The direction of massage is to be towards the groin of the body. The genitals should always be protected while doing the massage.

Along with that, the neck, shoulder and back massage will reduce your stress in no time. Listen to a pleasant music while doing the massage is always a better idea.

You can take help of your partner to do this. This habit will surely increase the libido which is lacking in many of the couples. The entire body massage will increase the blood circulation in your body, relaxes your body, and regulates the reproductive hormones.

By the entire process of the massage, you will get benefitted. So, make this as a practice and include it in your daily routine. Make sure to do this in the morning so that you can make a fresh start of your day.

Many kinds of toxins in your body are removed by the process of massage and thereby your body will be able to produce a very healthy content of sperms.

Along with the body and thigh parts for the massage, the important one is the head massage. The results are amazing when done daily or at least for 3 times a week. Stress will be completely shed off from your body.

All the hormones are regulated. It's very important to keep the brain and body healthy. So add the head massage in your list always. You can use coconut oil for the head massage.

Have a warm shower after the massage. The relief found by doing this is just feels good. This is a good practice to increase the Sperm Count Naturally.

12. STRESS

Stress is the main culprit in the male infertility. Even if a person has no addictions and no bad habits, he is susceptible to male infertility if he has over stress. The mental condition is very important to be fertile for an individual.

The brain is the main stream for all the reproductive hormones. If a person has over stress whatever it may be, by the mental problems of his personal life, family, relatives, job & occupation or any kind of stress if he is carrying in his mind, then his health is out of his way.

This is the major thing to declare one's health status now days, it can ruin your general health affecting your body along with the reproductive health.

When a person is in high stress then the body has high levels of stress hormones which affect the brain to lower all the required hormones for the body normal function which includes the reproductive hormones too.

Hence by the effect of this, brain function is hampered to maintain the health of the body along with the reproductive health. Brain is unable to send the proper signals to the genital organs to function properly.

In turn the function of the genital organs will be hampered reducing the levels of testosterone. The production of the sperms will be altered leading to the Lower Sperm Count.

This would be the pathology of your body by the reason just because your mind status is not good. Hence it's your responsibility to be happy and keep your mind calm.

You need to try all the means to reduce your stress because not only this, it can cause many other adverse effects on your body like increasing the cardiac health issues etc. The important thing is to go for once counseling and solve all your mental problems.

Practice the meditation daily in order to calm your mind. Spend time with your loved ones to boost the energy in you. It's very important to do pranayama the yogic practice which surely relieves all the stress in you.

A person suffering from Male Infertility already will be thinking a lot regarding "How to combat this situation & to father a child". This tension in your mind will put additional pressure which is not good.

But the truth is that if you leave all your tension regarding the infertility problems and lead a happy life, then it's possible to boost your fertility naturally as all your hormones are regulated.

If you are really stressed out by the job chart then take a long holiday leave, to make your health good. It is because as always priority should be given to your health even leaving your job or changing your profession doesn't matter in this regarding.

Stress is very powerful in causing the neuroendocrine issues to lower the spermatogenesis in you. Hence practice all the stress relieving measures for 2-3 months and focus on your health and then if you check the sperm count in you, you will surprised at your results and the reports.

You can really increase your Sperm Count this way naturally.

13. DIET

The male infertility is listed in the lifestyle disorder because the diet and the foods that we are eating in this generation is completely changed when compare to the food and dietary habits that were taken in decades back people.

It's as very simple as if we leave all the faulty dietary habits of this generation and if you could go back to our previous generation and habituate all the eating habits then it's very simple to increase your sperm count naturally.

The inner meaning of the sentence is that this generation has a lot of the packaged foods, junk food habits and all hybrid variety of the fruits and vegetables.

All the food we eat is probably doing at least a little harm to our body. It's our responsibility to change these eating habits even if not completely at least partially. You need to cut out all the bakery foods, junk foods, road side foods, packaged foods and processed foods.

Eat natural as much as you can. Be closer to the nature; make sure to select the naturally available foods. We are now much aware how food is adulterated in the market.

Hence choose and select the actual things by having good knowledge. Before you go for cooking the vegetables make sure to wash all of those properly in order to take off the pesticides that were sprinkled over. The chemicals attached to most of the fruits can be sperm killers.

You need to add more veggies in your diet. The green leafy are the most crucial in boosting ones fertility. You have all the required components in leafy vegetables.

It's very important to take the dry fruits like cashew nuts, almonds, walnuts etc. They are helpful in increasing the sperm count.

Add on the whole wheat and grains into your diet. Avoiding the red meat and consuming high sea food like fish may give you the required omega-3 fatty acids. You can have a better motile sperms by consuming them.

Researchers found that the people who take trans-fat more in their diet have decreased sperm concentration in them.

Men should avoid the soy products as it contains the phytoestrogens in a high amount. Make choice of the organic foods over other while choosing as it is beneficial to your overall health.

It's very important to take the food as required to your body according to your digestive fire. Don't over eat all the foods which could decrease your digestive capacity.

It's very important to maintain your digestive fire to give all the nutrients out of all the foods that you eat.

The Black gram is like a boon to the male. People who are really suffering from any kind of semen problems and sperm issues, they can take a single drug recipe i.e the black gram.

The well-known herbal drug which is very simply available in every ones kitchen is described in the Ayurveda to increase the sperm count.

Along with that it could increase the sex drive in an individual acting as an aphrodisiac, it deals with production of more motile sperms.

It helps you if you have any kind of premature ejaculation. All you need is to simply make a dry roast powder and make a sweet like payasam by adding pure cow ghee, rock sugar and milk. It really boosts your fertility.

All these diet changes will help you to increase the Sperm Count Naturally.

14. YOGA & EXERCISE

Your body should be fit and healthy in order to maintain a proper brain function and all other issues. You can combat with many health issues just by practicing yoga and exercise.

There are many yogic positions and asanas that can help you to increase the sperm count. For instance, the ***Badda konasana*** which resembles the *butterfly pose*. It helps to stretch the muscles of the inner thighs, genital parts and the hip area. Also the blood flow to the internal genital parts is increased.

The important **Bhujangasana** is also helpful in this concern. It resolves the premature ejaculation problem in the men. This asana helps to relax the body & mind. You can practice it for a good spine and healthy back muscles.

The third one is the **Naukasana**, the *Boat pose*. This asana surely helps you to correct the Erectile Dysfunction problem in men by just promoting the blood circulation to the pelvic area. It is very helpful to maintain the health of the male reproductive system.

The **Halasana**, the *plough pose* requires a little practice for a regular work out. It is very important in clearing out all the obstruction in the tracts of the genital system.

Hence it is crucial in maintaining the sperm quality. There by it boosts the male fertility.

Next one is the **Sarvangasana**, in which the whole body you should try to lift up over your chest. It is very important to stimulate the thyroid gland which is very important to maintain the normal fertile condition of the person. It also strengthens the back muscles, corrects functioning of all the organs in the body.

The **Sethubandasana**, the *Bridge pose* is easy to perform if you are the learner. You can practice it to boost your fertility in a very short span of time.

The ***Ashwini Mudra*** involves the contraction and relaxation of the pelvic muscles. It is very important to follow in a regular basis. It gives you a horse like energy, awakens the kundalini energy and strengthens the pelvic muscles. The sperm count is rapidly increased by this mudra. Anyhow this mudra is very easy to perform by anyone.

If you can't perform and practice these asanas, then it's simple to follow one idea. You can just perform the ***Surya Namaskar*** every morning. This composition of different positions is just enough to make your body fit and to release all the needed hormones in a right way and to boost your energy.

If you're not interested to do any kind of these asanas then don't get disappointed. You can even perform any classical dance to any kind of classical music every day.

It's just as simple as relieving your stress and making fit your body at a stretch. ***Aerobic exercises*** are good to perform to maintain your cardiac health. Any kind of zumba dance or simple exercises can help you in this concern. The excess body fat will be shed off making your body ideal.

 Exercises, yoga, dance will improve the blood circulation, decrease the fat and obesity, main line of choice for a good sexual life, to increase sperm count naturally and to be fertile.

15. MEDITATION

The importance of meditation is well known by the people of this era. Many people are getting aware of the benefits of the meditation in various conditions. You can get a doubt, how this could help to increase the sperm count.

Here is the answer; Meditation is the key to success in maintaining the mental health, stabilizing the stress and all the mental problems. It calms down your mind, improves the brain function.

When the brain is unnecessarily thinking about lot many things then the brain can't concentrate to perform the bodily functions properly along with the reproductive function.

So if you practice the meditation in a regular daily basis, then the issues that have been worrying you can easily get out of your mind.

You can get better results if you could practice mediation and pranayama in a calm place or any lonely place by keeping any chants like **Om** or **Om Namah Shivaya** or any of your favourite chant or song or music.

Already researchers have found that the meditation have its effects to boost the sex drive and to increase the levels of the testosterone in a person if he is a regular practitioner of meditation.

Also when you silently meditate, you will concentrate on your breathing and also you will learn to breathe properly with your mouth closed for a long time in a healthy way. This period of healthy intake of air and respiration will clear out much of the stress, gives you a pleasant sleep.

You can't expect what a good sound sleep can do it to your body. Many of the mind disturbances can be cleared out. You can focus on your reproductive life.

The peasant thinking related to be a father creates a positive energy in you which regulates the bodily sex hormones. You can just observe the change within no days of starting the meditation.

Many of the male sexual problems can be solved by the effect of the mindfulness. Many of the doctors, researchers, psychologists are treating their patients with a home based therapy of mindfulness in order to treat the sexual problems like Erectile Dysfunction by this method.

They are getting many positive results by following this. As some of the reproductive issues have the psychological causes as a primary reason, the meditation has been really a miracle in these kinds of cases in increasing Sperm Count Naturally.

16. IDEAL WEIGHT

In this generation other major cause that is ruining your sexual life is the obesity and probably the overweight. The obesity surely disturbs your sexual and reproductive life.

As the condition is the main reason for many kind of illnesses in the body like the Hypertension with High BP, diabetes, Hypercholesterolemia and etc, it is also responsible for the low levels of the testosterone hormone in the body.

Overweight damages the blood vessels of the body by doing the generalized inflammation in the body.

It is the main reason for the Erectile Dysfunction for the obese person. This condition makes him impotent and thereby starts the infertility problem. The back muscles and the big belly cause discomfort for a happy life.

Also the increased fat percentage in his body decreases the male active testosterone hormone and increases the oestrogen, the female hormone in his body. It is the main reason that causes infertility in him. The sperm count is drastically decreased thereby.

Excess weight may also hamper sperm production in body & causes a low sperm quality. The weight of the person is inversely proportion to sperm count in cases of obesity.

If you have an increased weight, then the fertility chances are very low but if you maintain an ideal weight according to BMI i.e if you lose weight, then your fertility chances will automatically boost up.

Men should check their BMI and maintain an ideal weight. The viable sperm count is also very low in the cases of obesity.

Researchers have found that the Leptin hormone which is secreted by the fat cells in an obese person is the responsible agent to damage the sperm cells in his body. Also due to more fat, there are possible chances of an increased temperature in his scrotum which in turn causes the damage of the sperms along with hampering the new sperm production, the spermatogenesis.

So, hence by the diet management like limiting the high fat content in your daily intake and by increasing the fibre content you can just slow down the deposition of fat in your body.

You can also opt to shed off the excess fat in your body by perspiring a lot in a day by increasing the physical activity like exercises, zumba dance, aerobic etc. whatever suits you.

Reducing your excess weight is a good way to increase sperm count naturally.

17. ANTI-OXIDANTS

The role of anti-oxidants is just like a miracle in cases of male infertility. When studying the male infertility, it was noted that the defective sperm function is the primary reason in most of the cases.

In general as a normal physiological mechanism, the seminal plasma of a person contains certain anti-oxidants in it naturally in order to protect the spermatozoa against the damage that could be caused by the oxidative stress in the body itself.

But due to some reasons like obesity, pollution, chemicals, drugs, etc., the anti-oxidant mechanism is lowered in the body there by increasing the oxidative stress leading to high damage to the sperms.

As a result, men are facing the defective sperm function because their normal function has been deteriorated. The sperm quality has been decreased which in turns causes the male infertility.

The damaged sperms can't help the man in impregnating his partner. The sperm count will be drastically decreased in no time. So the answer is clear, we need to increase the anti-oxidants in our body to protect the sperms and their quality. So replacing the anti-oxidants has been the first step in treating the male infertility in these days.

Some of the phyto compounds are very rich in anti-oxidants. You need to select those and have it to increase the sperm quality.

Some of the anti-oxidants are the vitamin C, Zinc, Vitamin A, vitamin E, vitamin B-12, etc.

It has been studied that the serious cases of severe low count cannot be improved by this method but cases of subfertility with moderate sperm count can be improved by these anti-oxidants.

If the root cause that is causing oxidative stress can be removed and tried with these products, then the results will be promising. These compounds help in neutralizing the ROS species which are very important agents in causing the sperm damage in the body.

 Opting for anti-oxidants is a good idea. There are many naturally available anti-oxidants along with many formulated one that are available in the market.

Some of the Ayurveda drugs have these anti-oxidant properties in it and are working great in these cases. You can choose any one to increase your Sperm Count Naturally.

18. ZINC

Researchers found that the zinc is very crucial in the spermatogenesis. Zinc is a mineral that is very important in the normal function of the male reproductive system.

It helps in the spermatogenesis, the sperm production part along with the sperm maturation process. The zinc concentration is directly proportional to the Male Fertility.

Any kind of the Zinc Deficiency is associated mainly with the gonadal dysfunction.

It can also affect the size of the testis. The zinc supplements can support the sperm formation and sperm maturation.

Some studies show that the zinc concentration in the seminal plasma is directly related to the sperm count, sperm motility and sperm morphology.

Zinc is the natural anti-oxidant in the semen that protects the sperms against the damage from the oxidative stress.

Zinc also possesses the anti-bacterial properties and acts as an agent in protecting from the infections.

Zinc is also very essential element in maintaining the lining of the reproductive organs in the male.

So, as the importance of the zinc is now very well known, the intake of zinc rich foods and adding the zinc supplements can boost your fertility and also helps you to increase the sperm count in the people with male infertility.

The zinc rich foods include the nuts, legumes, fish and meat which are very easily available. You can now boost your sperm count naturally by the simple remedies and foods.

19. LOVE

LOVE, has a miracle effect in the Male fertility. Now days it has been a mechanical life, not only in concerns of the occupation but also in means of reproduction. The sexual life should not be considered a routine job and should not be a mechanical.

We see many couples treating for the infertility get stuck when the doctor advices but with no feeling or no Love. This should not be the protocol. Instead you should allow Love makes things to happen.

Be in a relationship with your partner, show care towards her. She is not just a child making machine for you. She needs your Time, Love and Care. Being together will also increase the sex hormones.

The actual meaning of Love is.....
"Love should be into the eyes but not between the thighs" (credit; internet)

Many couples have a much decreased libido now days and suffer from it a lot. They are in search of boosting the libido ways both in male and female.

In order to boost it, you should opt the natural ways rather than the over the counter drugs or medicines.

Always choose a right tract or path. Love can create miracles. Leave the normal routine mechanical life and then take time to spend moments with each other for some days and then check the change in you people both.

The feeling of being together will surely boost your fertility hormones naturally that are required to get your reproductive health back in a better way.

So don't spare it as an unnecessary tip. Accept the fact and try it once.

20. SLEEP

Last but not the least; Sleep is an important factor that can increase the sperm count.

Researchers have found that the people who are deprived of sleep due to any kind of reason like the job or occupation that needs your work all the night time making you to spend the night under the artificial light or the long daily routine hours of sleepless nights by watching television or chatting with a friend unnecessarily or just as like a habit, those people will have a very low sperm count as their reports say.

Whatever the reason the people who are not getting enough sleep, especially the dark effect of the night, then the hormones are really imbalanced.

It's because, sleep is a wonderful opportunity to relax your body all the night under the moon effect, to repair your body by its specific night hormones.

But if you spent sleepless nights, then night hormones won't get a chance to repair your body. Hence it causes imbalance in your body.

All the systems in your body are disturbed along with the reproductive system.

Brain function is disturbed totally. So in order to resume your brain activity properly, you need to take proper sleep all the night at least for 8hrs.

Study shows that a proper sleep is associated to boost Men Fertility by increasing the sperm count, motility and the sperm morphology too.

Sleep decides your overall health. It releases all your stress. So, people who go to bed earlier have a better sperm quality.

This is a good natural way to increase your Sperm Count.

Guidelines for the Sexual Life

- Act in the early morning (around 4.30am) after a good sleep will have a higher concentration of sperms in the semen.

- Avoid mating during no moon day and days before and after.

- Always count the fertile days of your partner and then be together for a baby.

- Never have intercourse during the periods of your partner.

- Never choose another woman other than your wife.

- Always chose natural fruits and vegetables over street junk food.

- Do exercise properly and maintain ideal weight.

- Always wash fruits and vegetables to take off the pesticides.

- Build your immunity and get low risk of diseases.

- Expose to sunlight and get proper vitamin D

- Quit alcohol and Quit smoking

- Quit drug and substance use.

- Avoid unnecessary medications for simple illness and try to get over by natural immunity.

- Limit your exposure to pollutants.

- Limit your intake of soy and other phyto oestrogens as they can reduce testosterone.

- Make sure to get folic acid supplements.

- Avoid processed meat.

- Always choose a prone position while trying (male).

- Love your partner.

Ayurveda Drugs to Increase Sperm Count

1. ASHWAGANDA

Aswagandha, the *Winter Cherry* drug is an important drug to boost Male Infertility. The root powder is mixed with milk and taken to enhance the fertility.

2. KESAR

The *saffron* is well known drug to increase the Sperm Morphology since ancient days. The drug can be taken in a daily routine in cases of Defective Sperm shapes and size.

3. MASHA

This miracle drug, the *Black Gram* is very easily available in every kitchen and is very essential drug to maintain the reproductive health of the Male by its aphrodisiac properties. It also helps to increase the sperm count and motility.

4. JATIPHAL

In Ayurveda this drug was explained as the best drug in Premature Ejaculation. For the people who have their semen falling out very earlier to the act and face infertility problems, they can add the Jatiphal powder in their daily intake.

5. GOKSHURA

The Tribulus is well known drug that has been used since olden days for the male infertility. The fruit is potent enough to cure the urinary infection too.

6. SHILAJITH

Shilajith is a sex tonic which rejuvenates one's body and increases the core energy in a person. It clears out all the impurities of your semen and is responsible to increase the sex drive in men.

7. KAPIKACCHU

It is commonly called as the monkey tamarind, *velvet bean* or kauch.

The seeds of it are the useful part in this concern. It rapidly increases the sperm count along with the motility. The formulations with kauch are frequently recommended in male infertility by the Ayurveda practitioners.

8. MUSLI

This Ayurveda drug is very efficient to maintain the sex drive. The dried roots rejuvenate ones reproductive system. In cases of impotence, its use just does the miracles.

The safed musli drug improves the volume of the semen, increases the sperm count and motility.

9. SHATAVARI

This Ayurveda medicine really helps in the spermatogenesis in the body. The drug reduces the heat in the body there by helps in the sperm production. The powder is added to milk and can be taken.

10. VIDARIKANDHA

It is a starchy tube which is explained to increase the sperm count and in the illness of prostate issues. It increases the sperm quality and the sexual activity too.

Hope the Tips, Guidelines and Ayurveda drugs information helped you to gain knowledge regarding the *"Ways to Increase the Sperm Count Naturally"*.

Thank you for reading.
Have a nice day.

Keep smiling......it costs you nothing....!!!

Please give your feedback to us;
drchittymanthena@gmail.com

* 9 7 9 8 6 7 7 5 6 1 9 7 9 *